VILNIUS
02-09-10

Reprobate / GobQ Books
Portland, Oregon
2019

Darlinghurst Funeral Rites

Mark Mordue

The images in this book have been reproduced with knowledge & prior consent of the artists concerned, & no responsibility is accepted by the producer, publisher, or printer for any infringement of copyright or otherwise, arising from the contents of this publication. Every effort has been made to ensure that credits accurately comply with information supplied. We apologize for any inaccuracies that may have occurred & will resolve inaccurate or missing information in any subsequent reprinting of the book.

10 9 8 7 6 5 4 3 2 1

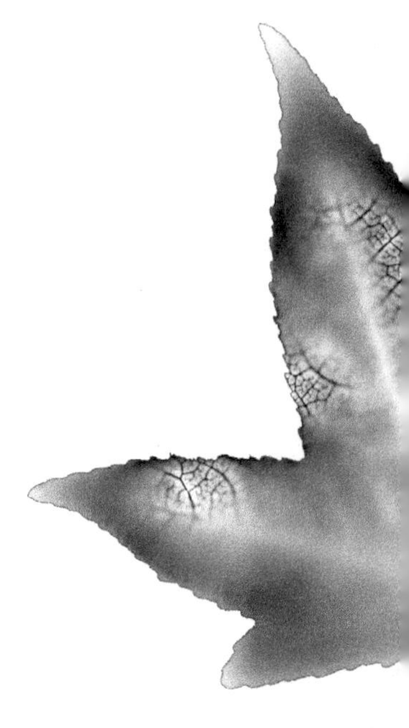

Darlinghrst Funeral Rites / Poems From the South Coast / Phone Poems (a flip book)

THIS IS A REPROBATE BOOK PUBLISHED BY

GOBQ BOOKS   ISBN 978-1-63587-869-1

$14.00

International distribution: Ingram Spark

Digital Edition Pending

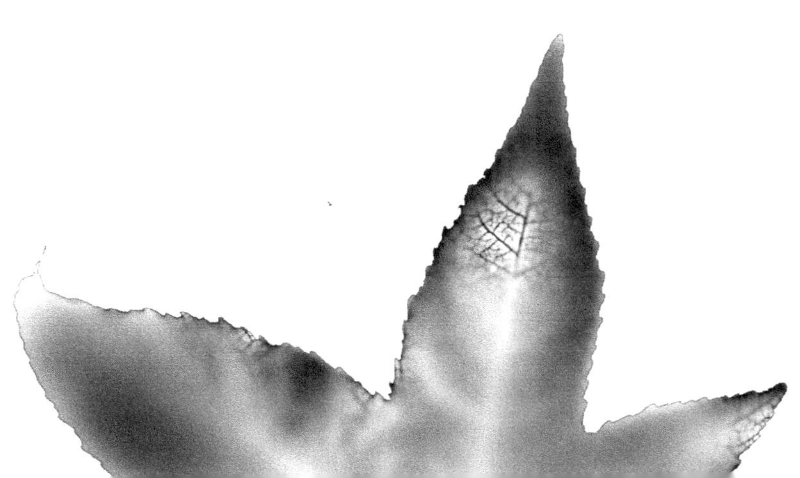

Editor: M.F. McAuliffe

Darlinghurst Funeral Rights Cover Photography: Michael Shay

Cigarettes: Chris Hatfield

Design & A.D.: T. Warburton y Bajo   Portrait of M. Mordue: Hugh Stewart

Solarized leaf: M.F. McAuliffe

Darlinghurst
Funeral
Rites

Contents

Darlinghurst Funeral Rites #1

I'm going white again
pacing Forbes Street in the weighted sunlight
all that sandstone, my weak shadow
we'll be inside soon, and shelter
until the moon is in the sky
drainpipe jeans and mirrors
voodoo paintings scratched from photographs
hello doom, your smile is ash so near us.
I'm late for the lines I never speak.
It feels right this laughter or so it seems
freighted by the night now and free
I might climb three storeys of a building
helter skelter just to fuck you. In time we will
do it in the gutter and be surprised by summer,
this wild wanting, this age, these eyes.
Sometimes I think luck is now my number.
But it's dice and Byron's lie that eats me.
Soon I'll limp from the blow-up,
all your Chagall dreams down the plughole.
Toy babies every one of us. Half ghosts,
dirt on their faces. *Ocean Rain.*
I still love you anyway. Glass in our noses.
The night in our veins. Free. We were free.

Horizon #1

Well, I'm driving cross the Harbour Bridge
Bright blue summer quite a vista
Opera House and Harbour smooth
Every girder cracking sun to diamonds
I want to make this city mine
Be a king do it right find a sister
And on into the true and pretty thriving
Till I am home and I have kissed her

All that glitter on my windscreen
Guitar sketches burn my radio
Swear to God lips to my rosary
I'll dream myself into a novel
Miss my family travel solo
Strive to keep my halo on
Poems are at my steering wheel fingertips
Yeah I'm alive to this scene's horizon

Wind in my hair paint my skull electric
My whole bedroom is inside the boot
Remain in Light is in my wrists. Africa!
Traffic lights! Highways! Skyscrapers!
Soon I will select my height and raise my fist.
Say it! Say my name. City. I'm a dreamer.

Strange Moves

I was just out of school
when one of my best friends
put a gun to my head
saying he wanted me to know
just how it was
and what he was feeling

He was training to be a cop
after being kicked out of the navy
getting way fucked up on macho

the guy I used to know
who'd played me Dylan's *Desire*
fast receding from the blow

We'd laughed about his brother
trying to kill me at his 18th
with a bow and arrow kit
us all shit-faced on keg beer
in the wide green-night backyard
ducking and weaving beneath hidden stars
like animals who would never get hit
while his brother brooded in the blackness
and we called out his toneless name

Now I see the family destiny in violence
like something my friend could not deny:

So there we were at 21
a lot of water gone below our bridge
he was the cop now
and I was the rock 'n' roll writer
but we were nothing
kids with working masks
scared of our own faces

He pulls that gun from his sock
and puts it to my head
and the party stops
and all that hash I smoked
down the side of the house with Luke and John
left my skull
like smoke through a whale's spout
death clears your head

Strange thing was how calm I felt:
youth keeps its own music
in the muscles of your moves
as I reached up and held his wrist
and then he cried
"I've been so frightened, I'm just so pissed".
Strange things. Strange moves. Skinned.

Jeepster Blues

"Super – cali – fragilistic
Expi – ali – docious
Even though the sound of it
Is something quite atrocious…" The way you sing it
then you laugh
On our stoned Monday afternoons
Your blue mini skirt, I'm 22
And I don't know to kiss you

The spooky rain, the Mambo Sun
You're as skinny as the motion of a deer
How was I to know I'd leave my home town
And travel one hundred miles to be near
A girl called Margot with a wide mouth
And a dream to be a puppeteer

A hundred visits, all those hash cakes
I was just a puppy off his lead
The bones of your body, o how I love you
"You were built like a car o yeah"
Marc Bolan had it right sweet thing:
I saw your hubcap diamond star halo

And later on when I heard paler news
That you'd spent a decade on the gear
Well I doubt I was a first thought,
Or a second either, but I thought of all your promise
The way anyone with eyes would love you
And then I shed a fragilistic tear.

Newtown Station Sunset

Hey man, maybe we can meet
on the platform at Newtown Station,
watch that tree that looks like it's falling down hill,
a wild fruit tree: pears, apples?

The light is always misty or dark,
our bodies slicked and pointed
while the tree holds on for dear life.

My California Poppy, my suede Doc Martens:
I wanted to look like John Cale, Velvet Underground era,
or Neil Young when he was doing 'Cowgirl in the Sand'.
You looked like a down-at-heel English Lord,
your hair like *Highway 61 Revisited*,
a poet without a poem I'd guess later on.
Too much cool just ain't no good for people.

You say you have a present for me,
something I might understand:
"If it doesn't appeal to you now,
I hope you will read it later
And think of me." Then you press it
into my hand. A book called
Voyage into Solitude,
a lone candle burning on the cover,
a lonely attitude, divine,
as if someone were previously present before us
weaving their own sunset out of wax and flames.

A very soft rain has begun to fall like a sheer curtain
so light the wind makes it look as if it is raining upwards.
The yellow wattage of the station bathes us and expands
out into the growing night. This world is breathing us in.
A train is coming. I feel the heat in my hand. A book: a ticket.
My shirt back is damp. We're leaving. We're leaving. We're fire and
we're rain.

Sorry Is Not A Word

The scenes are jumping:
I'm driving a white Toyota Crown
You're licking my face
We want to see a band
That's promised $10,000
To the first fan who hangs himself in town

One headlight up, one headlight down
We read 'the Enemy' we worship pills
Sometimes I think we will eat ourselves

Old men with plastic fists line the walls
They hate our hair they hate our smiles
The club vibrates with coins and lemons
And cards with queens and jack o' hearts
Metal ashtrays, glowing bottles, hair so blue
You'd swear an octopus was in our minds
When we walked into this room and grew

We are future lovers, full of premonitions
The sounds we make are glass and Africa
Nerves and romance, flowers, speed, German roads,
There's heroin and jazz, Iggy Pop and David Bowie
And from a rope our lives do swing, and not a soul is sorry

"The wind in our hearts, the wind in our hearts…"
One day we will fold up our lives like a paper aeroplane
But now we're parked outside the club

We're kissing. And from across the river
We can see the coming Braille
The smell. The change. The rain.

Beatified

Fingering the record racks at Ashwood's:
Buying John Lee Hooker's *This Is Hip*,
Television's *Adventure* on red vinyl,
And *The Lamb Lies Down on Broadway*.
Second hand, mint condition, twelve bucks total.
All three albums under my arm like a sign,
Walking up Oxford Street, wet as a river.
The sky has stopped and laid itself down
In a streaming hush: today feels a little unreal.
A picture rain-bowed into greasy gutters, oil and chrome.
Girls eerie and cruel and uncertain are parading.
The 'Walk' button jammed. Traffic pain.
Somebody has melted the cars into bullets
Then pressed the slo'-mo' on my executed brain.
I got my first St Vincent de Paul suit on,
The arms of the coat are too short,
Beautifying my wrists like Tom Verlaine.
It's midday and all the gay guys
Are coming out of dark, thumping pubs,
Squinting and red faced and grinning,
Their mouths trailing smoke behind them
Little gargoyles of ether that just float away.
Maybe I'll go have coffee, pick up a foreign book
From Nicholas Pounder's at the Cross,
Stroke the first few pages at the Tropicana,
And wait for a girl as pretty as bones to see me.
Offerings between us: a sugar spoon, steam,

Someone's else's cigarette, eyelashes, pepper,
Yesterday's ash in a tray, focaccia, lips, scripts.
The radiation of Dostoyevsky's *The Possessed*
Running all the way from my fingertips
To the unexpressed nation whispering
Sweet nothings into my spooky ear

Storybook

I call out to your window light
It's late and it's okay.
You lean on the sill
And call back from what seems
Like a terrace house watch tower:
"Hi, I'll come down and let you in."
We're not afraid of anything,
Least of all each other
And being ourselves.
We kiss in your doorway.
The night is clear and cool
We are written in its ink.
Your voice is scratchy and beautiful
Like seed husks. Like stars. Let's live together now.

Black Laces

He smiles at me and says I need your laces
We're so damned out of it
Each one of us has changed our faces

The car could be a bug; it might be a muscle
The accelerator cord has snapped
And thus and thou for you our hustle

To tie together all our shoelaces
And rope them to the engine's racing
The bonnet shut but not tight closed
As off we sail like yachting freaks
Down the great Pacific Highway

I'm tugging on those shoelaces like a tiller
G's at the wheel playing Ahab in cravat
It's not a pun to say were highly strung
But we really found a rhythm after that

I'd let the black line drop gently back to front
He'd shift a gear; I'd pull the thread again
I was speed, and G was all momentum
Amphetamine + dope = our new combustion engine

Between us was a line misspelled
A friend easily named 'Time'
So dubious and charming
His lace was fine and ragged

We'd raised our eyebrows and laughed at him
Before we wove it in
Less out of faith in its holding force
Than the highway sign that set our course
All hands on deck at dawn again!

Rock 'n' Roll #1

R-r-r-r-r-r-rock 'n' roll
Beer and speed and you
Trade Union Club games of pool
2nd floor warm up, cool shadows
Chalking every blunted cue

Pokies [1] chinging down below
All that smoke, the stench of stairwell
'King Ink' spilling down each concrete step
There's only one floor left to go

Who remembers anything?
There must have been a show?

The Moodists, Nico, Kill the King,
The Birthday Party's demon, cowboy heat?

Upside Down House, Sunday Painters,
John Cale's freezing, lonely scream
His downbeat hangman's dream
Of Elvis in a prison cell

'Heartbreak Hotel'
The story: never leaving

Folks we drowned in the mourning glory
Of dark blue bells that keep on ringing after this

1) *poker machines*

The slow stroke of a guitar and someone dimly singing
Embers that we took in while we thought that we were breathing
Through a winter of deceiving and spot-lit discontent
Electric warriors caught inside a spell of wherever the sound and
     fury went

Redheaded Lover

Redheaded lover I remember you
How great you looked in jeans
How far too many guys wanted you
The wooden floor of where you lived
Your hands and fingers like rope
Your great ass, your hippie heart
The songs you loved like little rays of hope
The frangipani tree outside your home
The strange way you believed in me
Redheaded lover, kind as one white flower
I was young and cruel and frightened
I did not know I was in love with you
And like so much else that passes and passes
All I want to say is I was a fool
A frightened fool whose mind was rearranged
The night I fell in bed with you
And as the morning is tomorrow now
A heightened time is strangely real
Of how I laid with my redheaded love
And not a word I said.

The Ocean (Nervous)

I'm nervous, I want to fuck you.
I'm nervous, I want to fuck you.
I'm nervous, I want to fuck you.
On this night. Here. Below stars.
The ocean is close. Let's do it.

Darlinghurst Backwards Spells

"Strawberry girl", lounge room bang,
then out we go now from Redfern snow
laughing like Goth orangutans
all our leather, all our torn jeans
full of go and smoking pot
at Catherine's house we invent our lot
a 'Christine' blast, a total gang,
all things move fast, then faster still
the times we were great and then were not
Dead Andrew in his leopard coat
Tim charming in his dusty state
Tanya's cockatoo-like flaring feathers
Graeme's red handkerchief: there was no weather.
We lived inside a room a while
and then we lived inside another,
I'm sad to say we forgot our sister
and just swapped her for a brother.
Tiny envelopes cut from fashion magazines,
each fold towards the perfect powder,
we went white, mere ghosts of passion:
from Redfern to Forget It House
is roughly half an hour.

Album Cover

It must be 3 in the morning
And someone has put on 'Lady Godiva's Operation'
All the passion in the room spilling
And undoing. Upstairs a secret is brewing.
I'll be happy to let it come down.

Here below, across two rooms, people sway,
Dancing, rutting, laughing, reading,
A little coven in the middle frown
Attempting some pretend telepathy.
They'll make that novel float apart some day.
Every page will be a wing somewhere.
So much is imminent. Our end is singing.
We just talk and squawk our minds away.

Tanya has a drawing on the door: a dead sparrow.
Right now she's cutting Phillip's hair,
His speckled painting of Graeme leans
Drying on the stairs. Tim believes
He might just fly up through the ceiling.
Who need wings when you've got arms and hair?
There must be something magic in this droning air.
On a caved-in green lounge two people kissing.
Who are they? No one knows. Thieving love
Before our ocean eyes, the floor is drunk:
I think I thunk this vision splendid but really I got no idea.

Lucia and Brad have just arrived. Take a potion.
Here, let me light your index fingers, welcome.
Ellen has the photo snapped. While Lou and Mo conspire
With smiles to make such pure gravity out of men's
desire:
Painter girls, Matisse hips, Joy Hester lips,
My kiss will be goodbye. Goodbye my kiss that lingers.

One more brushstroke, please, let it pass through
Our varnished, nested hair. The artist deep inside of us
Looking on at bested friends and lovers, our dreams
unharnessed,
As Ellen pours a happy hex over another set of leaking
photographs.
Candle wax from the melting corner of her crooked,
burning smile:
The bare energy distorting through a worn-out speaker
And bleeding out onto a bootlegged album cover

The Wailing Wall

It's late. I slip out of the buttered light
Of Tim and Tanya's lair
Perched like something out of the 1930s
High atop the Hanging Gardens of Forbes Street.
Out I go, down the rickety back stairs,
Past palms potted, radios blaring,
Beer bottles gathered, television conversations,
Human constellations fading into sleep.
It's summer and there's a breeze.
It touches your skin and hair
Like something conscious and alive.
Without thinking as I open the metal door
And step out from the Gardens
Into Burton Street, I turn left
And end up walking down Darlinghurst Road
Towards Oxford Street. Shadows move.
Boys with lost radioactive eyes.
Leaves rattle like scorpions underfoot.
Cars with Commonwealth plates, [1]
Jags, Mercedes, BMWs, Rolls...
All slide by, their headlights like tongues.
Judges, businessmen, politicians,
Picking up twelve year olds.
The street is misery and darkness
And even in summer it feels cold.
All the lost boys. Snarling. Empty.
Evil and pain push into your chest

As you see them opening car doors.
Behind them the sandstone wall
Of East Sydney Tech keeps its
Prison garrison heights. Cracked black.
We know this scene. See it all the time.
We've nicknamed it The Wailing Wall.
In the morning when there's not much left,
Maybe one or two boys shivering,
Crew cuts, shorn lambs bashed by the night,
Newspapers flapping over like damp nothing,
I feel this need to make a sign.
To say I'm sorry for them all.
To stand with my face against the colony brick,
And beat my palm against the yellow stone.
To hit my hand in sorrow against The Wailing Wall.

1) These license plates identify luxury cars for the official use of the
Australian Prime Minister, senior cabinet ministers and members of
Parliament.

The Cat's Meow

We'd meet at your boutique
A little clothing shop called The Cat's Meow.
I'd tremble with our secret life.
We'd close the door. Kiss, fuck, gasp.
Excited to the point of suffocation.
Across the road drunks would still be sleeping
Beneath sickened palm trees with the bends:
In winter the morning sun saved their lives
On a median strip everyone knew as Gilligan's Island.
In sight of these drunks and Taylor Square
We played at our own marooned and comic disaster:
Your hips, the smell of you, scissors,
Patterns on paper, an iron, a worktable,
That tiny finger of a room where we found heat
Again and over; catching each other's breath.
On a side street in spring the trees
Turned so intense a pale green
It was like all the leaves were dosed in LSD.
We had other lovers. Every meeting
Was an assignation grasped, fled from
And repeated, yearned for: we fitted.
I see you crossing the street, feline steps.
I'm on a fence and it's hard to know
Where I will jump next. My Catholic slink, arching,
Purring, I see you. And yes I shake. The trees brighten
And I walk towards The Cat's Meow.

Queen Bee

Queen Bee you're in your element
Queen Bee with all your soldiers there
Black honey in every catacomb
Alone by instinct I am losing me.

The maze is rich, the pollen sweet,
But the hive's collapsing anyway,
Queen Bee I'm seeking other flowers,
I want to leave alive today

Queen Bee your throne is awful sticky
Your soldiers are all on their knees
Do what you like these last few hours
I'm setting out alone

Soutine Stink

Who's gonna throw God's mystery
like a hat into the ring?

I'm not even trying to be out of step
listening to *No Guru, No Method, No Teacher*
opening my head up to Rimbaud's poems
that soon I'll read alone on the beach –
she can't reach me and I can't reach her.

Once upon a time our love was a slide show
psychedelic forests and blood red water
one lost child when we began
and one missing shoe at your first altar

Your trembling wrists, your purple coat
your movie star hair forsaking damage control
your voice like sand and honey class
Auckland aristocrat with Soutine stink
dead fish and steak that's caked in blood
on a table as our visitors pass

la-la la-lah-la la-la la-lah-la
la-la la-lah-la la-la la-lah-la…

All My Dead Friends

All my dead friends
even those still living
they know what all this means.
I look at the lines I write
the jumbled, crazy scenes,
for all the hurt
a fool can tell I love you all.
I'd do it again.
We were learning to be human.
That's all.
One night among candles and books
I do hope every one of us can reconvene
And do pretty much what we always did.
Party. Love each other. Betray one another.
Find the next day.
And begin again.

Black Knievel

My old girlfriend calls me
After twenty years or so
To let me know a mutual friend was evil
I tell her we were just taking too much speed
That he was less a germ of Crowley
Than a mirror name of Black Knievel.
It seems to me she wants an absolution
For fucking then hiding in his wardrobe
While yet another friend reproached her revolution.
Knock, knock who's there? A doctor bleeding,
Shame all over his own end of the needle.
You think this shift of weight is something new?
Your painter's hand, your lost dream: not my load
So stop sucking on my ear for a rock
I threw that ring into the River Oxford
Lock and key on our glass house almost believable
Till I took off flying with the lowly
And left this salted silver earth as Black Knievel

Big Stars

We're still not dead
Despite all the killing I have brought to the page:
Our mirror is still lying on the table
The hall, small as it is, is still filled with thunder
We still sit on the lounge
With our backs to the barred window
Looking in on our world
Away from the street and an audience of floating heads.
What's that you say?
"Another fucking animal… the killing moon…
everything that flies is not a bird… I am the passenger"?
If we *were* singing songs,
The lyrics stuffed like rags in our ears,
Our mouths open, tongues bending
Each word backwards into a hieroglyph
You would see, yes, it was true
We were not birds.
But we were, nonetheless, emblems of birds,
Illustrations of cats, dancers fixed
In street-poster glue to walls.
All that motion so infinitely slow
Writ in hand-hewn Darlinghurst sandstone.
A black telephone rings with an answer
It's time to open the door and walk
The night has been wound down
      like a metal awning
        dotted with luminous splashes
        of paint.
Can you see us moving?

New Sensation

Bourke Street leaves are made of sunlight
Autumn is a killer made of joy
I'm alive and I have made it
The fight for my identity
An arrival that has me breathing in the breeze
It's as if my whole life is a new nation
As I walk a day I never knew existed
Ed Kuepper's *Character Assassination*
Playing in my ears like some lost but close relation
And all around me peace and traffic
Pavements buckled by the tree roots
Truth behaving as I tell the breeze
I'm alive. I'm alive. The day is young.
O thank you, God: A new sensation.

Kids (Psalm)

We were just kids
even our cruelty
petals on a moon in June
obsessed with definitions and mysteries
it's true we mostly wore black and blue
sometimes you might think
we were made of tar and stardust
our true selves ankle-chained
to the ghosts of convicts
and the oracles of New Poetry
I figure it's so:
we were spat
from the diamond mouths
of Michael Dransfield
and The Saints.
Way ahead in the future
others will tread upon our stains
from Forbes Street through Taylor Square
all the way down Bourke Street
beneath an arcade of shivering trees.
We had a lot of fun in Darlinghurst
Till yes, it hurt my darlings.
In retreat, among the sorry hills,
a church bell rings. A priest sings.

24.1.

TANZ

Index of *titles* & opening/first lines

Also available from Reprobate Books & GobQ

& look for these Reprobate titles:

El Gato Eficaz /Deathcats, Luisa Valenzuela, tr., Jonathan Tittler (*en-face* bilingual ed.), ISBN: 978-1-93566-234-1

↖↗

A White Concrete Day: Poems, 1978 — 2013, Douglas Spangle (2nd. ed.), ISBN: ISBN 978-1-62847-660-6

↖↗

The Art of Waking Up: 62 Poems & a Song of Despair: Brenda Taulbee, ISBN: 978-1-63068-129-6

↖↗

$12

International trade distrib. through Ingram Spark

Ebook editions forthcoming through Google Play Books, Ingram Spark/Lightning Source, Kobo, Nook/Barnes&Noble.

↖↗ ↖↗ ↖↗ ↖↗ ↖↗ ↖↗ ↖↗ ↖↗ ↖↗ ↖↗

Look for special chappy projects with Iraq & Afghanistan & Somalia veterans & relief workers, Lithuanian & Croatian en-face anthologies, & other textual marvels from this fall & beyond

---

Gobshite Quarterly no. 13/14, Winter 2014/Spring 2014, $9

Gobshite Quarterly no. 15/16, Summer 2014/Fall 2014, $9

Gobshite Quarterly no. 17/18, Winter 2015/Spring 2015, $10

Gobshite Quarterly no. 19/20, Summer 2015/Fall 2015, $12

avail. online & through var. independent bookstores; issues #19/20 & after distrib. internatinally through Ingram Spark/Lightning Source POD)

Praise for *Dastgah, Diary of Head Trip*:

I JUST TOOK A TRIP AROUND THE WORLD IN ONE GO, first zig-zagging my way through this incredible book, and finally, almost feverishly, making sure I hadn't missed out on a chapter along the way. I'm not sure what I'd call it now: A road movie of the mind, a diary, a love story, a new version of the subterranean homesick and wanderlust blues – anyway, it's a great ride. Paul Bowles and Kerouac are in the back, and Mark Mordue has taken over the wheel of that pick-up truck from Bruce Chatwin, who's dozing in the passenger seat.

> — Wim Wenders, director, *Paris Texas*, *Wings of Desire*, *The Buena Vista Social Club,* and *Pina*.

There is a quick mind behind the open-hearted lines, lucid poetry with dark edges and sudden downward plunges. Although Mordue's subject is love, he is writing into the uncertain future, aware and willing to say what it feels like to live in the present moment, and to sing as he goes. These poems are gifts to the reader, a breakthrough into the open sky from the city's crooked back lanes and highways, a joy to read and experience.

> — Robert Adamson, author, *Canticles on the Skin, The Goldfinches of Baghdad, Net Needle*

The Australian culture of the 1980s derided tenderness in men. Mordue's vulnerability, receptivity to art and social injustice marked him as an outsider, and the resulting sense of otherness always colors his work. He is familiar with profound and contained suffering. One of Australia's truest beat poets, he is shaped by Walt Whitman, John Keats and WH Auden, and Bob Dylan, Marc Bolan and the Jam.

> — Antonella Gambotto-Burke, *The Australian*

Sydney's Darlinghurst, today prosperous and gentrified, was in the early '80s a jumpy skinsoup of amphetamines, sex and cacophony. Mark Mordue, who lived through those times, in an outburst of poetry and the fine tuning of a latter-day skill set, gets us there again. The raging glory has moved on, but is preserved here much as it was, thanks to his passion and guile.

— Douglas Spangle, author, *A White Concrete Day*

www.ingramcontent.com/pod-product-compliance
Lightning Source LLC
Chambersburg PA
CBHW051503050726
47593CB00005B/2212

PRAISE

FOR

Mark

Mordue

&

POEMS

FROM

THE

SOUTH

COAST

&

PHONE

POEMS

Few writers around are offering us journeys as haunting, evocative and distinct as Mark Mordue. Here is the rare poet not afraid of going his own way, regardless of fashion and convention.

— *Pico Iyer*

In these wonderfully generous, expansive and open-hearted poems Mark Mordue reminds us that the artist's first obligation is to make themselves vulnerable: to their pasts, to the world around them and perhaps most of all, to love.

— James Bradley, author of *Clade* and *The Resurrectionist*.

There is a quick mind behind the open-hearted lines, lucid poetry with dark edges and sudden downward plunges. Although Mordue's subject is love, he is writing into the uncertain future, aware and willing to say what it feels like to live in the present moment, and to sing as he goes. These poems are gifts to the reader, a breakthrough into the open sky from the city's crooked back lanes and highways, a joy to read and experience.

— Robert Adamson, author, *Canticles on the Skin, The Goldfinches of Baghdad, Net Needle*

Praise for *Dastgah, Diary of Head Trip*:

I JUST TOOK A TRIP AROUND THE WORLD IN ONE GO, first zig-zagging my way through this incredible book, and finally, almost feverishly, making sure I hadn't missed out on a chapter along the way. I'm not sure what I'd call it now: A road movie of the mind, a diary, a love story, a new version of the subterranean homesick and wanderlust blues – anyway, it's a great ride. Paul Bowles and Kerouac are in the back, and Mark Mordue has taken over the wheel of that pick-up truck from Bruce Chatwin, who's dozing in the passenger seat.

— Wim Wenders, director, *Paris Texas*, *Wings of Desire*, *The Buena Vista Social Club*, and *Pina*.

Poems from the South Coast

Phone Poems

24. I
TANZ

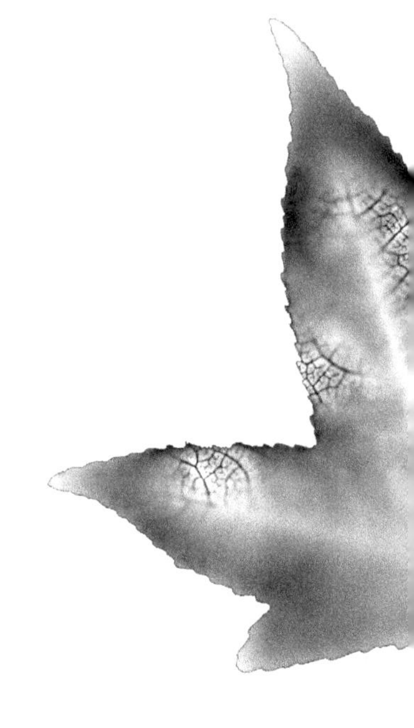

Editor: M.F. McAuliffe

Poems From the So. Coast *&* **Phone Poems Cover Photography:** Michael Shay

Mobile Phone Violence: Michael Shay

Design *&* A.D.: T. Warburton y Bajo   **Portrait of M. Mordue:** Hugh Stewart

Title page ref. photos: Mark Mordue   **Title page design:** T. Warburton y Bajo

Solarized leaf: M.F. McAuliffe

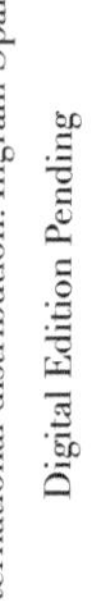

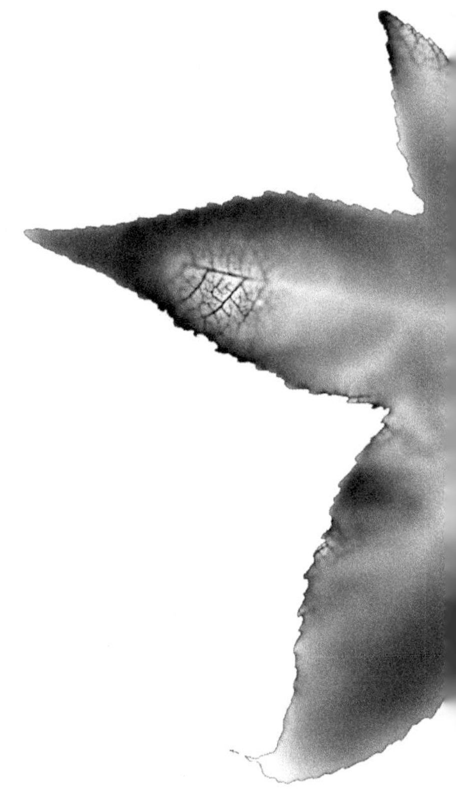

Poems From the South Coast / Phone Poems / Darlinghrst Funeral Rites (a flip book)

THIS IS A REPROBATE BOOK PUBLISHED BY

GOBQ BOOKS   ISBN 978-1-63587-869-1

$14.00

International distribution: Ingram Spark

Digital Edition Pending

table of contents

Poems from the South Coast

SILVERING

I'm stepping out into a world
I'm watching waves come falling down
I hear the kids on skateboard wheels
I see a tree bent to the ground
I play a song in praise of a crow
I taste the salt upon this breeze
I listen close to the Tasman Sea
I see a light on the water dark
I watch the breeze move through the leaves
I dream of flying across rocks and sand
I have my eyes and I have my hands
I'm going out through an open door
I'm thinking of this twilight here
I'm hearing waves that push then sigh
Another foreign light on a ship at sea
Ignites this world as it enters me

CORRECT COMMUNICATION

One day I will communicate
correctly with myself:
I will cross electrical wires with leaves
and hear the trees talking,
their words a spiky green
caressed by the wind's tongue
tasting of salt and a slate-coloured
sky on a rainy afternoon.
I will pick up stones from the beach
and ask who they are,
what dead men exist among them,
and if the stories are true:
that we walk over a graveyard
of sand and surf,
that the dead have been disinterred,
that a man from another time
has been set to rest again
in the long grasses nearby,
his magic a silent voltage
breaking the stones open
with a strange sorrow?

While the ships that sit on the horizon
wait for coal
and riders to the shore
feel the mercury swell
of every wave

coming and breaking and calling
back to the trees, back to the leaves,
the wind, the stones that once were stars,
breaking down here amid us
into pieces of who we think we are.

Some heavy joy running through
this world like electricity
saying 'speak to me'
'stop' 'breath' 'soft' 'help'
'cry' 'laugh' 'feathers' 'sick'
'love' 'home' 'lost' 'blue'
'children' 'magpies' 'shells'
'thunder' 'rest'…

WIRE LAND

In wire land the voices
hear as well as speak,
while clouds smoulder
off the escarpment
as if earth itself were cold air
waiting for a chance
to breathe itself in again,
the circulation
of sky and stone
its own communication
on the coal coast

where blackness is a virtue
and blue a way of dancing
and white a language
spoken to the living by the dead.
The trees shiver. The wind arrives with kisses.
Children sit by windows drawing.
Storm surfers pull moves from the skies.
A driver clears his windscreen with a demister.

ESCAPE ARTIST

One day there will be an escape
in silver and ink and spires of black green,
mobs of white galahs scrawking
wind ripples on a puddle
text on an iPhone
mind shimmer
trying to build a new surface
for a world going elsewhere.
Get in the car, find a new body,
the panic of these birds is only a sound
for gathering at dusk and departing
on this cold magenta evening.
Those galahs swoop up in clouds
of paper and bones
as if stoned by their own flight
onto slack electric wires.

A warm idling engine
shakes your stomach
while you sit
parked, door still open,
measuring a feeling.
Puddles look upward
at telepoles and trees.
A youth stands in a gutter
wearing blue reflector sunnies
as if he has just stepped
out of The Lost Boys
and on to a skateboard
that rattles like gravel
across your teeth.
The inhabited of this time
correspond and meet.
All things penetrate
and soak and chill.
I see magenta leaves sprout from the sharp trees. I deny I
    am in this
poem.
Cold rapture at twilight
turns me into someone else,
into a white bird, then a boy,
then a driver caught
behind his windscreen.
Looking is a way of being.
I am only like something:
I dissolve I dissolve I dissolve.

COME TO US

They will come to us in other forms:
smoke drifting from a chimney,
the backs of a mother and her son
as they cross a road slowly,
a Labrador from the house of the blind,
the knuckles of an old lady spotted
and lined like leather,
a row of unread books deep inside
the archives of a library,
a boy's voice on a mobile phone,
a rock pool filled with crushed shells,
the art of skipping stones,
a woman's poems about death,
the low flight of a magpie,
a child's painting of a desert…
yes, that is how they will come,
inside these things,
essences alight with feeling
for who we are and were
and seek to be,
the ghost singers of no-soul
and no-body
sirening us into never forgetting
that we pass through this world
  shape-shifting
       adrift
       strange
       as departing
mountain clouds

VIA DOLOROSA

The day that ends –
what burns it
from our hearts?
Who hurled the birds
in a crowning circle
over our heads?
The warmth now
is like honey.
My skin is golden.
I'd like to ride
on an old pushbike
with the wind
blowing at my back
cold from a green sea.
I'd like to ride
towards
the disappearing light
of this last afternoon.
The birds jab
and pulse
forming halos
in this sky.
The birds.
The birds
have lassoed
themselves
to my slowing breath,
and spill

like black
paper-cut tears
across the way.
All believers
must be
broken down
to leave
end of day.

HEAVEN'S GATE

A wet cool day
you're alive again
like the shrouded escarpment
dreaming of itself
sharp as the air
your jeans wet
legs clouded
a creature
60% water
designed for dematerialisation
inherently drawn to the sky
blood of mirrors and rain
bleeding you into the trees
feet slipping on pavement
leaves sodden
icy spirits

licking the skin
of the awakening road
walk this way
will and wisp
your soul unbeading
as a rosary downpour
heaven's gate
between telepoles
and the forgetting
of whoever
you thought you were.

HOPE YOU'RE OKAY?

I'm on the edge of the world today.
Maybe it's violent white
maybe it's branch black
maybe it's rattled
as if it all
were painted
on a window pane
and made to shake.
Don't let your heart
sink into the turmoil
of the wind and sea,
the beyond that deepens
this feeling
the world could eat itself
or glisten in its own
broken vision.
There's a meal at home
worth making,
steam over a bowl.
Children will talk
over a telephone
of trees falling,
and wires of light
crackling in water.
A warm shower
a change of clothes

a touch of hands
or hopes sent
will change things.
We are made
of vast flights
in the turbulence,
bridges as calm
and elemental
as a light turned
on again.
Turn to the maths
of love: the names
of family and friends
in communication
radiating as
a call accepted,
slices of light
against darkness.
Tonight you will
eat and sleep.
A bed, a dream,
a new silence
breathing over
the world inside you.

Phone Poems

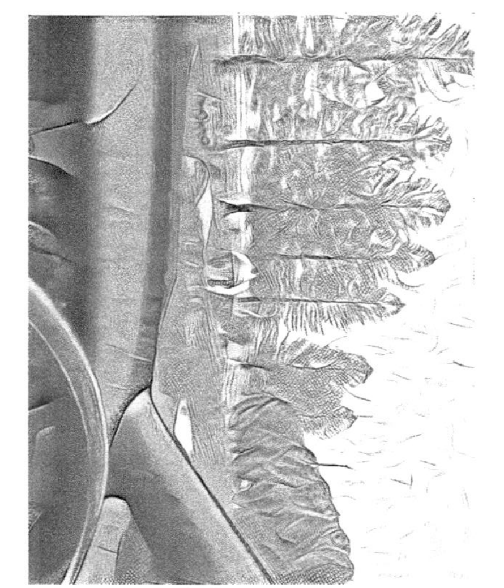

YELLOW MOON

Yellow moon,
yellow moon,
I look at you.
Your light is dust
as you rise.

THE VIOLINIST & HER

MOTHER

The violinist and her mother
sit in some disassociated tempest
on the slack metal
and hard blue vinyl
of a 7.35pm Inner West train.
Her hair curls out wild,
nervy and young,
from a high ponytail.
Her mother
has a severe bob cut,
modern, Newtown crisp
frazzled by a summer
that won't go away.

Neither speaks.
The daughter could almost
be happy,
some energy springing
through her body
confusing confusion
with joy. The mother
is pained, hands tied
like a gnarly brooch
from an art show.
She just wants a word
from her daughter,
a sign.
They are like one another
swimming in the mirror
of this carriage,
a silver sliver
of ash and voices,
twilight and relief.
Their station.
The daughter rises.
The train shunts
and stumbles,
its wheels kerning
on the rails,
entering your teeth
your nostrils
your gut.

The mother follows.
They leave
almost as if
they were strangers,
but an audience
applauds
their sorrows,
the delicate concert
of their tension,
their love
at 27 degrees Celsius,
invisible, human,
a minor suffering
that serves as
music to our eyes
to our hope-filled fears.

HOW IS THAT?

The big game
in the street:
there's a tennis ball
skinned,
a garbage bin,
K-Mart wickets,
an ice cream,
skinned knees too,
blood elbows,
what a perfect afternoon,
tears,
cheers,
someone's dad
half-pissed,
a mother
with a diamond
on her jeans,
a radio
squalling
"boys suck",
but even though
the girls control
that radio,
the boys on the street
disagree.
Are you out,
did you hit it for six?
I saw someone

catch a stone
the colour
of cream.
The girls start
turning cartwheels.
Sausages are burning,
kids gather like
a bushfire
growing.
The sky yells out
"I'm bigger than you"
but the kids
in shorts
with dirty t-shirts
say
how is that?
And the adults
sip their beers
watching their children;
a half of whom
they were themselves,
and a half so new
and fresh
and far away
there are not nearly
enough tears
to say how happy
this one day has been.

RAIN FOR ACHILLES
(CHRISTMAS EVE 2016)

Check myself,
check my darkness
at the door.
Familiar prayers:
my son's hand
in mine,
my daughter's thoughts
in pencil
on a wing,
my eldest son
touching a ball
with his foot
and moving forward
as if about sing.
How about this day?
I watch my sons
catch a bus
to the movies
and they throw
silhouettes
across the windows
at my heart.

The texts
of my daughter
scroll like poems
down and deep
through my eyes.

I'm sweating
Christmas shopping
weighs me down
my feet hum
with stone pressure:
the world heats me!

I'm Achilles
escaping Coles
not dead
reincarnate
as an Inner West father
my chest
still half full
of ashes
from my first burning
and the dark blood
that rose
from loving hard
and loving hard
again. Now
here I am
with a plastic
shopping bag.

I'm in a war
against my own
culture
and what it does
to my children.
I can't win,

the story
is written,
but I fight anyway
unable to cool
my anger.
An arrow comes
inevitably
and I lie down
in a memory
I wove
to give myself
some peace.

And there
I wait
for the surviving
bright
powerful
love
of my children
to recall me
from an afternoon
dream I had
of a field
where strange
white animals
ate the grass
that grew above me.

The things
I saw

and continue
to see.

I seem
to only believe
in being.

Suddenly
it begins to rain
an early evening
burst
and all the air
tastes green
and sweet
on Christmas Eve.

Thunder breaks
in a wave.

I can feel the gap
in time
from where I woke
to speaking here
as if I
were lightning
and the guttering
runs
tender and violent
the constitution
of sounds
like my veins.

from **Return Journey**

It's so hot
there's an imaginary rain
spitting rare drops
you can almost feel
from the ripple
of the clouds.
Some ugly birds honk.
A siren blows and sighs.
The traffic sounds
like the sea.

LET IT GO
(MELBOURNE BLUES)

I had a sky blue
denim jacket,
$10 sunnies
made of green plastic,
a pair of worn out jeans
that looked like they'd seen
better days.
I was singing
to my headphones:
It's so hard to be a saint
in the city, Marquee moon,

Born under punches,
Cemetery gates, Dreams.
Yeah I was king.
I'd drunk red wine
like it was
my own blood
and my friends said
you should lay off
those bad American
vampire movies.
I looked at the girls
and their hair
was like
falling sand
or sheets of oil
shiny with desire
so close
it ran
right down
my nervous hand.
I looked up
at the buildings
shaped like waves,
I saw Elvis in silver,
I saw a pencil drawing
of the home town
of Ai Wei Wei,
I had a coffee

just after midday
at Pelligrini's Cafe
where the shelf
held
Robert Pinsky's
curled translation
of Dante's Inferno.
I smelt like sex,
I struggled,
I flew,
I thought of my eyes
as stones in a river
that pulled me back
to my children
and to my yesterdays.
I remembered
as it was so freshly seen
Ai Wei Wei's torture
the marble facts
of his spiritual dismembering,
brother Warhol's hair exploding
his obsession
with American death
how it stayed
all over me
after the exhibition
like something real.
Melbourne I visited you

to talk to a ghost
made of delta blues
and European veins:
true things happen
in disorder —
now I'm holy
and you can pray
for my body twice —
and if that's not me
then please
convey your sweet regrets
to the creature
acting as my host
down by the dirty river
where he cast my eyes
into the wind and light
and into my swallowed future
just to see
it flow away.

WHAT WILL HAPPEN?

What will happen
when I stop moving,
when I drink less
coffee grains,
when my back
stops really hurting
from the endless
time on trains,
when the library
forgets my fines
and then forgets my name,
when that feeling
of cold sand
on dog-run beaches
no longer
belongs
to part of me,
when the death
of waves
is not my music,
when telegraph
wires don't
string my sky
like crucifix guitars,
when the smell
of cut grass
is once more over,
when the flame trees

strew their seeds,
when the robot
chant of destinations
is a woman
I never knew,
when the lantern
is left rusting,
when the ships
return for coal,
when Brett Whiteley's
ghost
leaves the motel,
when Rob Younger
cuts his mane of hair,
when DH Lawrence
makes love to no one,
when the Clever Man
calls through
the coolness
of the stones
to place a feeling
on the moon,
when the streets
no longer hear
my footsteps
in the evening
walking home
from the train
back to Thirroul?

WALKING HOME

My boy
walking home
from swimming
with a towel
wrapped up
beneath his arm

My boy
with his quiet way
is already
turning into
a man

My boy
walks into
the afternoon sunlight
like a hero
in a movie
I cant begin
to imagine

or see

or fully understand.

My boy
is sweet with dogs
playing at his feet

is magic
with a football
darkens himself
with a hoodie

reaches out
and holds me
on rare days
that make me

feel lucky.

My boy
is sunlight
and freckles

and hesitation

he's an angel
on the pavement

and his back
fills
with beautiful wings

*from **Sitting Here***

I'm a poet inside a poet
inside a poet.

I'm an act of vertigo
in a long slow tune
after an afternoon sleep.

BIRTHDAY SONG

Singing a birthday song
I crossed the water
just like I did
thirty years ago.
Everything was blue
and sun split
the girders and cables
of the Bridge
like a bike wheel spinning.
Sails were white
in the wind.
I thought I was a man
but I was a boy
and it was summer
just like this
and the morning

sparkle of the sun
was as bright
and new as my heart.
I was all dreams
and when I spoke
my eyes turned black
and shone
like the moment
when coal
under pressure
glows and burns
and gives off
the diamond
premonition
of what it can be.
Speedboats
laced the Harbour
with white trails
of foam.
Men worked
with rope.
A fine young girl
stood at a railing
and looked out
and as the wind
trailed through
her red hair

I fell in love
with a stranger
then left my boat
and forgot her.
Thirty years
and here I am again
on the water
traversing my old ways
an inhabitant
of Five Bells
and it's chiming
surge from
school-time reading.
Almost disintegrated
like the egg andromeda
of a John Olsen painting
that trails ecstasy
and octopus ink
across the
seaweed soul
of my world.
I'm ready to step out
into being an old man
the yellow bouys
float a lazy warning
of the shallows
all the clouds curve up
as if they were hands

receiving something.
I see the stone green
headlands where ships
first came to look
and I feel
a curious sorrow
for what was here
as if the sandstone
held people still.
Seagulls scoop
the surface of the
water, heavy and moving.
Tonight the year
will measure itself
and we will shoot
lights at the stars
celebrating our sparks
our rose geometry.
My face is changed.
But I'm still here
undrowned
born to run
seeking
my young heart
in the water-turned
reflections
of the sun.

AMPHIBIAN

I walk slower than I'd like
I've slipped back in time
slipping slipping
for him for her
I'm as heavy as Jupiter
and no one can estimate
the moons I've crushed.
Apple juice
drying
between my fingers:
I think of when
I was a kid
watching sci-fi horror
the webbed hands
and the heroes
forced to turn
amphibian.
I've sunk below
the smooth black
footpath
and a child on a bike
in a blue shirt
rides right over me.
Golden leaves
brush my secret face.

Chalk marks
get on
my secret skin.
I'm as heavy
as Jupiter
and I keep on
reaching speaking
sinking.
Don't believe
the football
left to float
in the canal.
Don't believe
that falling leaf
turning over
and over
its colours
like it was burning.
Don't believe
the heart
with an arrow
through it
carved on a tree.
Believe in me.
I'm deep under
and I'm still shining.

KEEP IT QUIET (ICHTHYS)

I was fucking for the money,
I was fucking a ghost, rolling
in a thick cloud of something
like honey, I was made
of money and string
attached to everything,
puppet-like I was happy,
you know what I mean,
having been obedient
to incense and earth
I mistook unruliness
for rebellion, but the hook
in my mouth was amniotic bread,
and when I swam away
a fish into this great sea
of being average and no different,
I understood my own being,
my skin as silver as a door key,
my eyes looking sideways and ahead
of me. I was a creature not a seer.
I was a fish not a religion.
I was swimming. I was breathing water.
Seeded. Mouth agape. Needing food.
In the shape of a secret on a wall,
a scrawl of holiness in darkness,

please let the ones who know:
just head this way. Head this way,
follow me with candles and songs so hushed
you would not know them from the silence
in our hearts, our tombs, our Roman wombs:
it's a secret, it's a pendant, it's only me.

MOGADISC

Poems From The South Coast
Index of titles and first lines

Phone Poems:
Index of title & first lines